Snakes!

Deadly Predators or Harmless Pets?

by Sarah Houghton

Reading Consultant:
Timothy Rasinski, Ph.D.
Professor of Reading Education
Kent State University

Capstone Curriculum Publishing

Capstone Curriculum Publishing materials are published by Capstone Press,
P.O. Box 669, 151 Good Counsel Drive, Mankato, Minnesota, 56002
http://www.capstone-press.com

Library of Congress Cataloging-in-Publication Data
Houghton, Sarah, 1978-
    Snakes!: deadly predators or harmless pets?/by Sarah Houghton
    p. cm.
    Includes bibliographical references (p. 62) and index.
    Summary: Introduces the characteristics of snakes, how they are classified,
which are harmful to humans, what to do if bitten by a snake, and other facts
and fictions.
    ISBN 0-7368-9503-5 (pbk.)—ISBN 0-7368-4003-6 (hardcover)
    1. Snakes—Juvenile literature. [1. Snakes] I. Title.
QL666.O6 H836 2001
597.96—dc21

                     2001002989

Created by Kent Publishing Services, Inc.
Designed by Signature Design Group, Inc.

Photo Credits:
pages 4, 44, Michael and Patricia Fogden/Corbis; pages 6-7, Roger de la
Hope/Animals Animals; page 8, Gallo Images/Corbis; page 11 (right), 14, David
A. Northcott/Corbis; page 13, Kevin and Suzette Hanley/Animals Animals; page
18, Zig Leszczynski/Animals Animals; page 26, Joaq Gutierrez/Animals Animals;
page 39, Joe McDonald/Animals Animals; page 42, A. Desai/Animals Animals;
page 50, Richard Sobol/Animals Animals

Printed in the United States of America.

1 2 3 4 5 6 07 06 05 04 03 02

2

Table of Contents

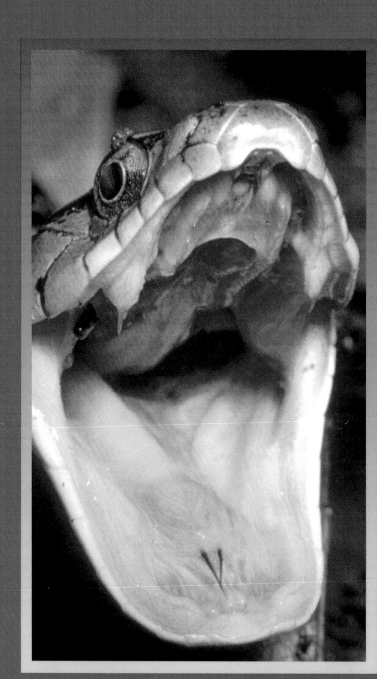

Toad-eating snake

CHAPTER 1

Snakebite!

You're walking down the road. You look down. Your heart stops. Frozen with fear, you see a snake coiled and ready to strike. You can't tear your eyes away. The forked tongue flicks in and out. The fangs appear. Do you scream? Do you run? Do you stand there and stare? What would you do?

What Do You Know about Snakes?

Many people are afraid of snakes. Maybe they have heard horror stories about snakes. Or they might have been bitten by a snake. Maybe snakes just give them the creeps.

But not all snakes bite people. Many snakes are harmless. It helps to know something about snakes. A little knowledge might even save your life!

---

coiled: wound into rings or a spiral
flick: to move in a sudden or jerky motion

Taken by Surprise

Lucas Sibanda was walking to work one morning. Sibanda lived in South Africa. He walked the same isolated path every day. Suddenly, a python appeared from the bushes.

The 57-year-old Sibanda was too surprised and frightened to move. He stopped dead still. This was a big mistake. Within seconds, the python had slithered up to Sibanda and wrapped itself around his body.

---

isolated: not near anything else; cut off

African rock python

Normally, snakes won't attack people unless they feel threatened. Sibanda had done nothing to threaten the python. He had just been walking to work. But now, he was under attack!

Sibanda had good reason to be scared. Pythons are constrictors. They kill their prey by squeezing it until it can no longer breathe. The python was ready to squeeze Sibanda to death.

---

threatened: in danger
constrictor: a snake that wraps around its prey and squeezes it to death
squeeze: to press hard; to exert pressure

Breathless

Pythons use strong muscles in their backs to constrict their prey. Every time the prey breathes in, the python squeezes tighter. Soon, the prey can't breathe at all. The python began to squeeze Sibanda in just this way.

Biting Back!

Mongoose with its prey

Trapped in the python's grip, Sibanda thought fast. Luckily, he remembered something about the snake's worst enemy, the little mongoose. The mongoose has razor-sharp teeth and lightning-quick moves. The mongoose will leap at a snake, bite its neck or head, and kill the snake.

---

constrict: to squeeze

The Winner Is . . .

There was only one thing to do. Just like a mongoose, Sibanda opened his mouth and bit the snake. He bit it just below the head, sinking his teeth into its scaly neck.

Sibanda did not stop there. After biting the snake, he kicked it and punched it with his feet and fists. Despite the squeezing, Sibanda finally freed himself from the snake's powerful grip.

But the battle wasn't over yet. Sibanda had to kill the python before it could attack him again. With a stick, Sibanda beat and killed the snake. He had escaped from the python's death-squeeze.

Lucas Sibanda bit the snake to save himself. But what if a snake bites you? If the snake is venomous, it can poison and even kill you. Read on to find out what one teenage boy learned about snakes the hard way.

---

venomous: poisonous

A Rhyme to Remember

In a Georgia pine forest, five 15-year-olds were camping by a stream. At dawn, the rain that had lasted all night finally stopped. The boys built a fire, cooked breakfast, and complained about the cloudy day.

Jack Gordon and Larry White took their breakfast dishes to wash in the stream. Near the wet bank, Jack slipped on soggy pine needles next to a big rock. He sat on the ground laughing at himself. Then he looked at Larry, whose eyes had widened in horror.

A stinging burn shot up Jack's arm. Only then did he see the red snake slither back under the pine needles. Jack had stepped on the snake when he slipped. The startled snake had bitten him.

Larry started shouting, and the other boys came running.

---

horror: great fear

As children, the boys had learned a lifesaving snake rhyme. Jack and Larry remembered it as the snake made its escape.

If red touches yellow, it kills a fellow.
If red touches black, venom it lacks.

The snake that had bitten Jack had red and yellow bands. Those bands touched. That meant it was the deadly coral snake. The harmless milk snake looks very much like the coral snake. Only it has red and black bands that touch. There was no time to lose.

Can you tell which snake is the deadly coral snake?

Poisoned!

Jack's attacker had been the deadly eastern coral snake. Jack was in grave danger. Two boys stayed with Jack. Larry and another boy raced to the ranger station nearby.

The ranger called an ambulance. Then he and the two boys hurried back to the campsite. Jack was calm, but his hand and arm were swelling rapidly. Where was that ambulance?

When the ambulance arrived, the paramedics checked the swelling in Jack's arm. Luckily, the other boys had kept Jack completely still while they waited. The medics had just enough time to get Jack to the hospital.

As soon as Jack reached the hospital, a doctor gave him a shot of antivenin. Antivenin is the medicine that stops snakebite venom from poisoning a victim. Jack survived, thanks to a quick response from his friends, the ranger, and the paramedics.

---

grave: serious, dangerous, or alarming
paramedic: a person trained to do first aid

Staying Safe

Lucas Sibanda and Jack Gordon faced death by snakes. Both pythons and coral snakes can kill. Fortunately, snakes normally won't attack humans unless they feel threatened.

If you see a snake, try not to scare it. Walk slowly and calmly away. Don't chase or try to capture it. Don't risk a dangerous encounter with a snake—even if you think you know what kind it is.

Some constrictors and venomous snakes are dangerous to humans. But most snakes aren't dangerous to us at all! It can be hard to tell a dangerous snake from one that is harmless. But just what is a snake anyway? What makes a snake a snake?

This Hogg Island boa looks peaceful, but it could kill you.

encounter: a meeting

Ball python

Chapter 2

What Makes a Snake a Snake?

Most people fear snakes because they don't know much about them. Others are scared because they know too much! Are you afraid of snakes? Why or why not?

Are All Snakes Dangerous?

Every year about 40,000 people die because a snake bites them. That's enough people to fill a major league baseball stadium.

But not all snakes are venomous biters or deadly constrictors. In this chapter, you will learn a few more "snake facts." You might even grow to like these interesting creatures.

Just What Are Snakes?

All snakes are reptiles, but not all reptiles are snakes. The following diagram shows traits that all reptiles share. It also shows traits that help to identify certain reptiles.

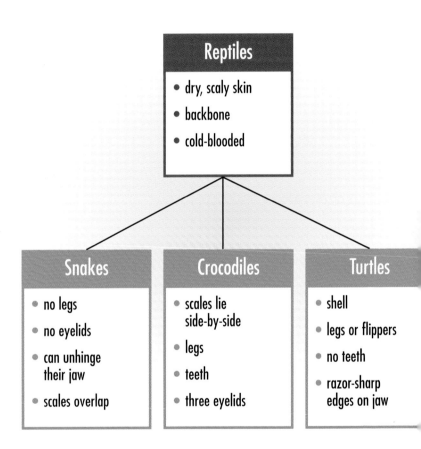

Reptiles
- dry, scaly skin
- backbone
- cold-blooded

Snakes
- no legs
- no eyelids
- can unhinge their jaw
- scales overlap

Crocodiles
- scales lie side-by-side
- legs
- teeth
- three eyelids

Turtles
- shell
- legs or flippers
- no teeth
- razor-sharp edges on jaw

trait: a special quality or characteristic
cold-blooded: animals that get their body heat from their environment

How Long Have Snakes Been Around?

The first reptiles lived about 340 million years ago. Their relatives include the dinosaurs, which evolved about 245 million years ago. Snakes are quite young for reptiles. They only evolved about 136 million years ago!

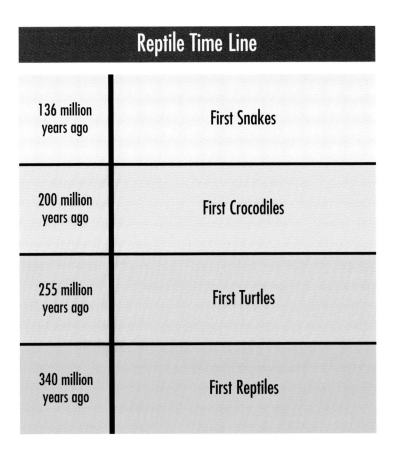

Reptile Time Line	
136 million years ago	**First Snakes**
200 million years ago	**First Crocodiles**
255 million years ago	**First Turtles**
340 million years ago	**First Reptiles**

evolve: to change slowly over many years

Are Snakes Slimy?

A snake's skin is made of scales. These scales keep snakes from drying out in the heat. The scales are made from keratin—just like your fingernails!

Some people think snakes are slimy. This is probably because some kinds of snakes produce an oily substance that polishes and seals their scales.

Snakes have something else in common with humans—both shed their skins! Humans shed small flakes of old skin and grow new skin all the time. Snakes shed all of their old skin at once. Before their old skin peels, snakes grow a new skin underneath.

A snake's old skin stretches as the snake wriggles free.

Where Do Snakes Live?

Snakes are found in many different places. Snakes live in deserts and rain forests. They live in forests and grasslands. Snakes even live in cities. You can also find snakes in fresh and salt water.

Snakes are commonly found in warm places. The reason is because snakes are cold-blooded. Cold-blooded creatures get all of their warmth from their environment. Snakes sunbathe and also take in heat from rocks and sand. In contrast, humans heat their body by breaking down and burning the food they eat inside their body.

Even cold-blooded creatures can get overheated. If snakes get too hot, they will hide under rocks to get cool. They also burrow down into damp soil or sand, or cool off in water.

This doesn't mean that snakes don't live in cold places, however. During the cold winter months, snakes hibernate.

---

burrow: to dig a tunnel in the ground
hibernate: to spend the winter in a deep sleep

How Big Are Snakes?

Snakes can be as short as 4 inches (10 centimeters). They also can grow to over 30 feet (9 meters) long.

We often think of snakes as long and thin. However, the girth of a snake can be over 3 feet (0.9 meters). Large anacondas can weigh in at 450 pounds (204 kilograms).

How Do Snakes Move?

Although snakes have no legs, they move around easily. They can glide along the ground, climb trees, and swim. Some even throw themselves through the air to move from tree to tree.

The backbones of snakes are long and flexible. This allows snakes to use a wavy or rippling movement to travel. Their scales help them grip surfaces. They push themselves along using muscles.

---

girth: the distance around the middle of something
flexible: not stiff or rigid

Four Ways Snakes Move

"S"-shaped movement

The snake wriggles from side to side.

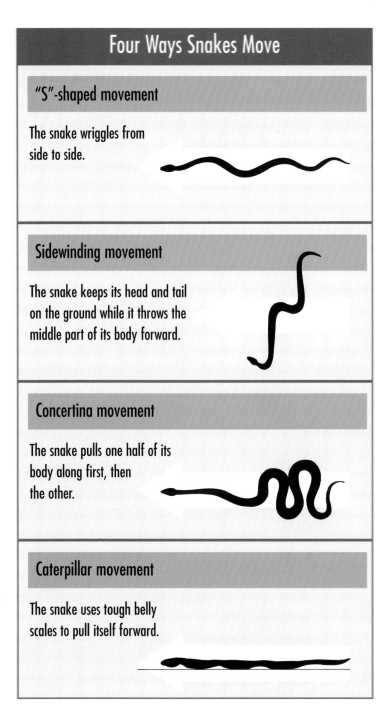

Sidewinding movement

The snake keeps its head and tail on the ground while it throws the middle part of its body forward.

Concertina movement

The snake pulls one half of its body along first, then the other.

Caterpillar movement

The snake uses tough belly scales to pull itself forward.

Should You Fear Snakes?

There are more than 2,500 types of snakes in the world. About 10 percent of these, or 250 types, are dangerous to humans. Snakes usually go out of their way to avoid humans. Normally, a snake will only attack a human in self-defense.

When in danger, many snakes try to warn and scare off enemies with a hiss or rattle. Some give off a terrible stink. Other snakes twist into small balls or knots. Some snakes bury themselves or roll over and "play dead." Snakes go to all these lengths just to avoid a fight.

Diamondback rattlesnake

Do Snakes Have Predators?

Snakes fall prey to a number of natural enemies. Many animals hunt snakes. Some snakes even eat other snakes!

Yet humans are by far the greatest threat to snakes. Humans threaten snakes in a number of ways. They may destroy the snake's habitat. Some humans hunt and kill snakes. Road traffic also kills many snakes.

What's Your Verdict?

All snakes share traits with other reptiles. That is, they are cold-blooded and have a backbone and scales.

Snakes come in many shapes and sizes. Some snakes can kill you, others are harmless. Most snakes fear us as much as some of us might fear them.

So now you know a bit more about what makes a snake a snake. Does that make you fear them more or less?

---

habitat: the place where an animal or plant naturally lives

CHAPTER 3

Venom

Has an animal ever bitten you? What kind of wound did the bite make? Have you ever seen a snakebite wound like this? It is not a pretty sight.

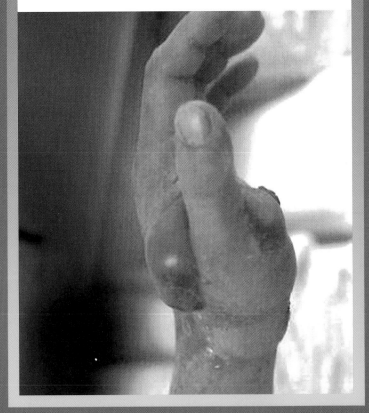

Snakebite wound

How Snakes Kill

Snakes kill their prey in several ways. Some snakes simply snatch the prey live in their mouth and begin to swallow. Constrictors, as you've read, squeeze their victim until it can no longer breathe.

Other snakes bite and inject their prey with poison called venom. Since snake poison is called venom, we say some snakes are venomous. The chart below shows one example of each kind of snake.

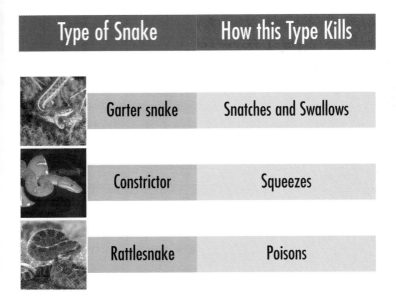

Type of Snake	How this Type Kills
Garter snake	Snatches and Swallows
Constrictor	Squeezes
Rattlesnake	Poisons

inject: to force or drive something into the body

What Does Venom Do?

Venom can affect a person in different ways. But all venoms stop the body from working as it should. Many types of venom cause pain in humans, and some venoms can kill.

Venomous Bites

Venomous snakes use venom to help them kill prey and to defend themselves. These snakes have fangs to bite their prey. They also have venom sacs that store their poison. These sacs can make a venomous snake's head look triangle-shaped.

Venomous snakes have hollow teeth. These teeth are needle-sharp. A snake's jaw has incredibly strong muscles. These muscles help drive the venomous snake's teeth into its prey. The venom travels down the teeth and mixes with the victim's blood. The victim's blood carries the venom rapidly to all the body parts.

What Big Teeth You Have!

Vipers have extra long fangs. They can inject venom deep into their victims. Because of this, the poison enters very quickly into the body. Gaboon vipers, like this one, have the longest fangs of any snake. The fangs can be up to 2 inches (5 centimeters) long. These vipers come from Africa.

fang: a long sharp tooth

Types of Venom

There are two main kinds of venom. One is a nerve poison that attacks the brain and central nervous system. It stops the victim's breathing or stops its heart.

The other type of venom poisons the victim's blood and muscles and destroys body tissue. Both kinds of venom can kill. Death can occur in seconds, or it may take much longer. The level of pain and speed of death depend on three things:

- the type of snake;
- the size of the prey;
- where on its body the prey was bitten.

Ten, Nine, Eight . . .

Green mambas live in trees. These venomous snakes swoop down on their prey in seconds. Mamba venom is very powerful. It can kill a person in 10 minutes.

---

tissue: any material that forms some part of a plant or animal

Paralyzing Prey

Snake venom does not always kill prey. Some venom only paralyzes the prey so it cannot escape. When the prey is paralyzed, the snake does not have to continue to fight it in order to kill it. The snake might squeeze its victim until it can't breathe. Some snakes even eat prey alive.

Painful Death

The venom of most American pit vipers affects the blood and destroys body tissue. This venom causes a painful death.

Most Poisonous

The yellow-bellied sea snake is the most toxic of any snake. There is no known cure for its poison. People bitten by this snake die quickly and painfully.

paralyze: to make helpless; to make something unable to move
toxic: poisonous; harmful

Venom from Copperheads and Cobras

Many bites are painful but not life-threatening A healthy adult bitten by a copperhead will suffer swelling and bleeding, but will not usually die.

When a copperhead injects venom, the poison breaks down the tissue near the wound. The venom attacks the body tissue from the inside, like acid might attack skin from the outside.

Copperhead

Cobras, the snakes usually used by snake charmers, raise themselves up to attack. This allows them to reach the eye level of their victim. Spitting cobras can squirt venom at their enemy. They aim for the eyes to cause pain and blindness. Then they are free to approach their victim or to flee.

Cobra

Dry Bites

Snakes have venom mainly to help catch food. It takes a long time for snakes to produce venom. Thus, many snakes control the amount of venom they inject. Sometimes people get a "dry bite." This is a bite where no venom is injected.

Even extremely deadly snakes usually don't inject enough venom to cause death in humans. In some cases, the victim suffers terrible symptoms. In other cases, the victim suffers nothing except a fright!

---

approach: to go toward
symptom: a reaction or feeling in the body

Treatment for Snakebites

Most snakebites can be treated. However, it is important to get medical care quickly.

People treat snakebites in many different ways. Some people stick to old, traditional ways. For example, some people take medicines made from snakes' brains. Others suck the bite wound, to try to get the poison out. They have to spit quickly afterward, though. If they don't, the venom may destroy the tissue in their mouth.

The best snakebite treatment is a shot of antivenin. As you've just read, different snakes have different types of venom. Each snake venom requires a different antivenin. That's why it is important to be able to describe the snake that bit you.

---

traditional: handed down generation by generation

Where Does Antivenin Come From?

Drug companies make antivenin. They create it by injecting tiny amounts of venom into animals such as horses. The animal's body makes antibodies to protect the animal from the venom. As this happens, more venom is injected. The animal gradually becomes immune to the venom. This means the animal's body becomes able to fight the poison.

Then blood is taken from the animal. The antibodies that fight the venom are used to make the antivenin drugs. The drug companies sell these drugs to hospitals and emergency rescue teams.

What Should You Do?

If a snake bites you, first call an ambulance or a doctor. Doctors can save most snakebite victims. If there's no phone, or if an ambulance can't reach you quickly, get someone to drive you to the nearest hospital.

---

antibody: a substance made in the body that can act against a virus or other foreign substance
immune: not affected by; able to resist disease; protected

What the Doctor Will Do

The doctor will give the victim a shot of antivenin. Only a doctor should inject antivenin. In some cases, patients react badly to the antivenin. This is called an *allergic reaction*. A doctor will know how to deal with an allergic reaction to the antivenin.

What Not to Do

The Red Cross gives advice on what not to do for snakebites.

DO NOT apply a tourniquet.

DO NOT apply ice.

DO NOT cut the bitten area.

DO NOT wash the bitten area. Venom on the skin will show what type of snake made the bite.

DO NOT let the victim move the injured body part. Movement spreads the poison through the blood stream.

DO NOT let the victim take his or her pants off if the bite is on the leg. Keep the leg still.

DO NOT give the victim any painkillers, such as aspirin, unless the doctor has just told you to do so.

tourniquet: a bandage twisted tight to stop bleeding

Can Venom Be Good?

Strange though it seems, some snake venom can help people. Using venom as a cure is not new. Some cultures have used cobra venom as a painkiller for a long time.

Certain types of venom can help some heart patients. A person's heart may beat too fast. This can be dangerous. Doctors may want to slow that person's heart rate. Certain types of venom kill a victim by slowing its heart rate until the heart stops. Doctors may be able to use just the right amount of that venom to slow a person's heart to a healthy rate.

Snakebite is a horrible way to die. Even if you don't die, you can get pretty sick or sore from a snakebite. However, snake venom may also be useful, even life-saving. As you can see, there is more to snake venom than meets the eye!

Corn snake

CHAPTER 4

Feeding Time

Imagine being eaten alive by a snake. Does it eat you whole? Or nibble on you bit by bit? Let's say it swallows you alive. What does it look like as you "tour" the snake's insides? What do you know about the eating habits of snakes?

Dinner with the Snake Family

Snakes are carnivores, or meat eaters. In the wild they have to catch prey in order to eat. But they don't always kill before they eat.

Depending on the snake, any animal from a tiny mouse to a large deer might be on the snake's menu. Some snakes eat birds, fish, or eggs. Some also eat other reptiles. Certain snakes even eat other snakes.

Most snakes swallow prey alive. Some kill or paralyze their victims first, however. Read on for more juicy facts about dinner with the snake family.

How Snakes Get Food

Snakes track their prey by sight or by scent. As the tongue of a snake flickers, it gathers scent particles in the air or on the ground. When the snake pulls its tongue back into its mouth, these particles enter what is called the Jacobson's organ.

The Jacobson's organ is two hollow sacs in the roof of a snake's mouth. These sacs have many nerve endings. These nerve endings are very sensitive to odors. Using its tongue and Jacobson's organ this way, the snake can detect tiny clues that prey is nearby.

The Jacobson's organ does more than just detect that food is around. It also lets the snake know exactly where the prey is. Then the snake can move in for the kill.

Venomous Killers

Venomous snakes use poison to kill or paralyze their prey. Some venoms target a certain type of prey. This doesn't mean that the venom won't harm other creatures, though!

---

scent: a smell left by an animal

Nonvenomous Killers

Boa constrictors are an example of nonvenomous snakes. They have no poison fangs. Boa constrictors rely on speed and strength to catch food. While they lie in wait, they often anchor themselves to a tree.

The boa constrictor seizes its prey with its jaws. It then wraps its powerful body around and around its victim, forming a strong coil. The boa constrictor matches the pressure of the coil to the breathing of the prey. Usually, boas kill quickly, without breaking bones. The prey simply suffocates. The boa then eats the dead body.

The strong coil of the boa constricts around a mouse.

---

anchor: to hold in place; to become fixed
suffocate: to stop from breathing

What Snakes Eat

Observing snakes in the wild is not easy. Much of what we know about how and what snakes eat comes from zookeepers and owners of pet snakes. These people have observed what snakes like to eat and what keeps snakes healthy.

Like all other living things, snakes need certain types and amounts of food to keep them healthy. People who keep snakes must feed them exactly the right foods, at just the right times.

The chart on the next page describes the different kinds of food snakes like to eat.

A red-necked snake eats a lizard.

Food Recommended for Snakes in Captivity

Type of Snake	Best Type of Food
Boa constrictor Python Rat snake	Rats, mice, birds, and rabbits. Some will eat small lizards and other snakes. Young snakes prefer smaller creatures.
Garter snake Water snake	Fish, frogs, toads, salamanders, earthworms, and slugs. Many will eat mice if they are covered with fish or frog mucus.
Indigo snake King snake	Mice and lizards. The indigo snake will eat anything if hungry, even cat or dog food.
Racer Vine snake	Lizards, mice, and bird chicks. Young snakes will eat crickets and grasshoppers.

captivity: the state of being held prisoner
mucus: the thick, slimy substance that coats the inside of the mouth, nose, throat, and other parts of the body

How Snakes Swallow Food

Once a snake has killed its prey, what next? A deer can make quite a feast. But snakes cannot chew. How do they go about eating?

Imagine trying to pass a dog, or a small deer, through a drainpipe. Snakes often eat animals that are much bigger than the snake itself is. But how do they do this?

An Indian python swallows a deer.

A snake can dislocate its bottom jaw. In other words, it can move its jawbone out of the normal position and out of the way. This allows the snake to swallow large animals. With this jawbone, the snake can open its mouth wide enough to fit around its prey. Then it can pass the prey from its mouth into its body. The special snake jaw also helps drag dinner into the snake's mouth.

Snakes also can push their windpipe forward. This allows them to breathe while eating. If a snake could not do this, the prey would cut off the snake's breathing.

Once the food passes through the snake's mouth, the skin of the snake's throat stretches. This allows the food to pass through the snake even though it has not been chewed.

---

dislocate: to come out of its usual place
windpipe: the tube in the neck that is needed for breathing

How Snakes Eat Eggs

Certain types of snakes only eat eggs. Eggs are much easier to catch than animals. But what does a snake do with an eggshell?

Some snakes just crack open the egg with their teeth and eat what's inside. Some egg-eating snakes have no teeth, however. These snakes swallow the whole egg. Then, special spines that stick out from the snake's neck bones break the shell open.

The egg makes a large bulge in the snake as it moves along the snake's throat. As the neck spines break the egg, the shell contents pass into the snake's stomach. The shell

itself is forced forward, back to the mouth. The snake gags and brings up a pellet of shell.

Egg-eating snake of South Africa

pellet: a little ball of packed material

Good Eaters!

One South American boa survived for 16 months without a meal. It got thinner, but it did not suffer. Now that's a diet!

You might think snakes have pretty gross eating habits. Snake table manners are certainly different from our own. But there are still stranger facts and fictions about snakes. Do you know any weird snake stories? Read Chapter 5 to find out more.

A green snake eats a cricket.

Banded sand snake

Cold-blooded Facts

What is your favorite "snake fact" so far? What fact has most surprised you? What questions about snakes do you still have?

Amazing and Weird Snake Facts

Snakes are pretty remarkable. But we're not through with them yet. In this chapter, you will discover even more amazing and weird snake facts. Here is one fact to get you started.

More about Snake Tongues

As you know, the snake's forked tongue can't hurt you. The snake uses it to pick up scents of prey or enemies. Also, a male snake can follow the trail of a female snake by using its tongue and Jacobson's organ.

---

remarkable: worth noticing; unusual

Still Deadly after Death

There are many mistaken beliefs about snakes. Some of these beliefs contain a kernel of truth. For example, people used to claim that snakes never died before sunset. Some legends held that no matter how badly injured, a snake would remain alive until the sun went down.

In fact, a snake's body may continue to move after its death. Just as chickens may run around after their heads are chopped off, snakes twitch long after death. The freshly severed heads of snakes have bitten and killed people. The head is not alive, but the nerves still respond to touch. This twitching led people to think that snakes waited until night to die.

---

kernel: the most important part
twitch: to move or pull with a sudden jerk
severed: cut off

Look into My Eyes

Another false belief is that snakes can hypnotize people. This idea might have started because snakes stare fixedly. However, snakes have no choice. They have to stare because they can't blink! Snakes have no eyelids.

A snake seems to have a glassy stare because it has no eyelids.

hypnotize: to put into a trance
fixedly: without blinking

Charming Snakes

Snake charming has long been practiced in both India and Asia. The snake charmer plays a pipe and a cobra rises from a basket, swaying to the music. People believe the snake is hypnotized or even dancing to the music.

In fact, the snake can't "hear" the music at all. Instead, it feels the vibrations. Rising to defend itself, the snake follows the moving pipe. It matches the pipe's movement sway for sway, in case the pipe decides to attack.

Snake charmers in India

---

vibration: fast movement back and forth

A Very Bad Idea

Although it is highly risky, some people try to make themselves immune to snake bites. They inject tiny amounts of snake venom into their bodies. Little by little, they increase the amount. Over time, their bodies might build a strong defense against the venom. Often this goes horribly wrong, however. People have died terrible deaths from trying it. Venom is a dangerous poison.

The Fastest

On land, the fastest snake is the black mamba of Africa. This snake can move at about 10 to 12 miles (14 to 19 kilometers) per hour. The black mamba is also one of the deadliest snakes on land. Mamba venom can kill a person in 10 minutes!

Hide and Seek

Despite their size and strength, pythons will hide rather than attack a human. Sometimes, the python can't escape, however. Then it has to attack. A human usually is no match for the suffocating strength of a python.

The Most Dangerous

The boa constrictor lives in Central and South America. This tropical snake can live from 25 to 30 years. Once these boas grow more than 10 feet (3 meters) long, they are a threat to all but the biggest wildlife. Boa constrictors kill even large animals by suffocating them.

Emerald tree boa

Bad Eating Habits

Captive snakes do not get along well at feeding time. Sometimes, two snakes will grab the same prey. Neither will let go. Eventually, one snake eats the other, swallowing it down, still attached to the other end of the prey!

Feeding snakes in captivity can also be dangerous. A hungry snake might grab any food it sees. That "food" might be the human keeper. Big snakes have overpowered their owners at feeding time.

Snakes usually swallow prey headfirst. They do this so the victim can't attack them if the victim is not quite dead. Sometimes snakes cough their food back up—still alive!

A northern water snake eats a frog.

Mastigodryas snake

Fascinating, Beautiful, and Lethal

Okay, so snakes might not be the best dinner guests. And while they are fascinating creatures, some of them also are lethal. A snake can be both a beautiful pet and a deadly enemy.

Being bitten or caught and squeezed by a snake is rare, but it does happen. Understanding more about snakes is one way to avoid danger. It might even save your life.

Finally, always remember, there is more to a snake than meets the unblinking eye.

---

lethal: deadly

Epilogue

Strange but True "Fact Bites"

Nature's Warning

Most venomous snakes are brightly colored or make a rattling sound. This is nature's warning!

Big Bite

King cobras sometimes kill Indian elephants by biting them on the trunk.

Caged Up!

The record for a man staying in a cage of venomous snakes is 60 days. Was he crazy, brave, or stupid?

Backward Teeth

The emerald tree boa has long, sharp, backward-pointing teeth. The teeth help the snake to grab hold of its prey and stop it from escaping.

Two-headed Snake

The Steinhart Aquarium in San Francisco, California, once had a two-headed California kingsnake. The two heads sometimes bit each other.

Old Bites

The older the snake, the worse its bite. (Moral: Ask the snake its age before you let it bite you.)

King of the Snakes?

The California kingsnake eats other snakes—even poisonous rattlesnakes.

Deadly Snakes of the World

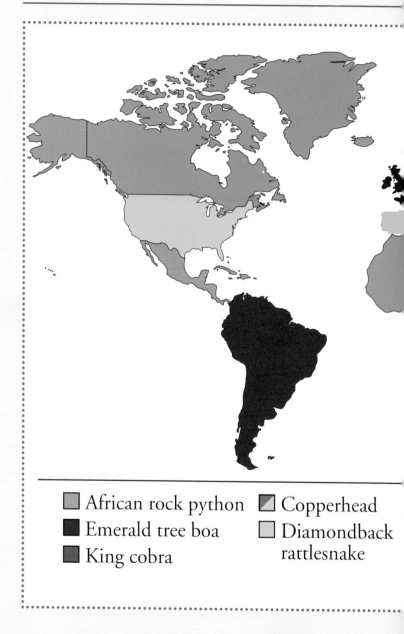

☐ African rock python ◪ Copperhead
■ Emerald tree boa   ☐ Diamondback
■ King cobra   rattlesnake

Coral snake
European adder
Gaboon viper

■ Green anaconda
■ Black mamba
■ Vine snake

Glossary

anchor: to hold in place; to become fixed

antibody: a substance made in the body that can act against a virus or other foreign substance

approach: to go toward

burrow: to dig a tunnel in the ground

captivity: the state of being held prisoner

coiled: wound into rings or a spiral

cold-blooded: animals that get their body heat from their environment

constrict: to squeeze

constrictor: a snake that wraps around its prey and squeezes it to death

dislocate: to come out of its usual place

encounter: a meeting

evolve: to change slowly over many years

fang: a long sharp tooth

fixedly: without blinking

flexible: not stiff or rigid

flick: to move in a sudden or jerky motion

girth: the distance around the middle of something

grave: serious, dangerous, or alarming

habitat: the place where an animal or plant naturally lives

hibernate: to spend the winter in a deep sleep

horror: great fear

hypnotize: to put into a trance

immune: not affected by; able to resist disease; protected

inject: to force or drive something into the body

isolated: not near anything else; cut off

kernel: the most important part

lethal: deadly

mucus: the thick, slimy substance that coats the inside of the mouth, nose, throat, and other parts of the body

paralyze: to make helpless; to make something unable to move

paramedic: a person trained to do first aid

pellet: a little ball of packed material

remarkable: worth noticing; unusual

scent: a smell left by an animal

severed: cut off

squeeze: to press hard; to exert pressure

suffocate: to stop from breathing

symptom: a reaction or feeling in the body

threatened: in danger

tissue: any material that forms some part of a plant or animal

tourniquet: a bandage twisted tight to stop bleeding

toxic: poisonous; harmful

traditional: handed down generation by generation

trait: a special quality or characteristic

twitch: to move or pull with a sudden jerk

venomous: poisonous

vibration: fast movement back and forth

windpipe: the tube in the neck that is needed for breathing

Bibliography

Cooper, Paulette. *277 Secrets a Snake Wants You to Know.* Berkeley, Calif.: Ten Speed Press, 1999.

Ernst, Carl H. and George R. Zug. *Snakes in Question: The Smithsonian Answer Book.* Washington, D.C.: Smithsonian Institution Press, 1996.

George, Linda, James Martin, and Mary Ann McDonald. *Boa Constrictors; Cobras; Copperheads; Coral Snakes; Cottonmouths; Garter Snakes; Pythons; Rattlesnakes.* Snakes. Mankato, Minn.: Capstone Press, 1996, 1998.

Mattison, Christopher. *Snake: The Essential Visual Guide to the World of Snakes.* New York: Dorling Kindersley, 1999.

McCarthy, Colin. *Reptile.* Eyewitness Books. New York: Dorling Kindersley, 1991.

Montgomery, Sy. *The Snake Scientist.* Boston: Houghton Mifflin, 1999.

Parsons, Alexandra. *Amazing Snakes.* Eyewitness Juniors. New York: Dorling Kindersley, 1993.

Useful Addresses

The Reptile Trust
1-3 Busty Bank
Burnopfield
Newcastle Upon Tyne
NE 16 6NF
England

Reptile Rescue
2025 Guelph Line
Suite 187
Burlington, ON L7P 4X4
Canada

Steinhart Aquarium
California Academy
of Sciences
55 Concourse Drive
Golden Gate Park
San Francisco, CA
94118

Internet Sites

Discovery School's A-to-Z Science
http://school.discovery.com/homeworkhelp/world
book/atozscience/s/516260.html

General Information About Snakes
http://www.thesnake.org/general.html

Snakes
http://www.sandiegozoo.org/wildideas/animal/
snake.html

Index